Common Sense of a Different Kind:

Matter-of-Fact Thoughts on Women and Dating

By
Megan A Frost

My little book is dedicated to all who read this, to those of you who encouraged me to share this with the world, to my fellow author Mrs. Cary Frates, and to my family…

Dad, Mom, Bryan, David, Aaron, Grandma and Grandpa Lizotte, Grandma and Grandpa Frost, Gisela and Wright Cowger, Michelle, Tami, Sue, Mary, Liz, Grace, Donna, Christina, Jeff, Scotty, Mark, Julius, Rody, Ron, Tobe, Bruce, Greg, Jenny, Aimee, Justin, DeAnne, Timothy, Jeff, Tessa, Kelly, Pat, Collin, Morgan, Alex, Mira, Momo, Emma, Kane, Billy, Stacy, Annie, JT, unborn baby 1, unborn baby 2, and unborn baby 3…

…who I love deeply.

WS Sonnet XVIII

Evelyn: An inspiration to me, an
inspiration to all and a Sonnet for us to
remember and share.
I love you.

****

Text copyright © 2008 Megan A Frost

Frost, Megan A
Common Sense of A Different Kind:
Matter-of-Fact Thoughts on Women and
Dating / by Megan Frost

Summary: These thoughts divulge why I
believe women torture themselves with
what should be dating/relationship/male
common sense.

ISBN 978-0-6152-1173-2

Contents

One
The Gist
* 1 *

Two
All About The Author
* 3 *

Three
Setting the Stage
* 6 *

Four
The Games We Play
* 11 *

Five
You're Not Five Anymore So Stop Pretending
* 15 *

Six
The Red Flags Are Your First Chance to Walk Away
* 25 *

Seven
Prince Charming Who?
* 31 *

Eight
Holding On to a Broken Relationship
Won't Change the Fact that It Is Still
Broken
* 39 *

Nine
Don't Waste Time on Another Women's
Future Husband
* 44 *

Ten
The Non-Fixables
* 54 *

Eleven
Where Has All the Confidence Gone?
* 59 *

Twelve
Making the List
* 67 *

Thirteen
The End
* 70 *

Fourteen
My Final Thoughts
* 74 *

Common Sense of a Different Kind:

Matter-of-Fact Thoughts on Women and Dating

The Gist

1

When Thomas Payne set out to write what is believed to be one of the most influential sets of historical writings in America, he boldly put on paper what the early pre-American colonialists believed, but never dared say aloud. When it came to his views on England's control over the inhabitants of this country prior to the Revolutionary War, Payne had no hesitation in voicing what he believed was our God-given right to freedom; in fact, he even went so far as saying that our very right to freedom was just plain ol' common sense. Unlike Mr. Thomas Payne's pamphlet, mine may never hold any historical significance, and might not change the course of history as we know it. However, inspired by Payne's *Common Sense,* it does champion the idea of common sense – but just of a different kind.

In a nutshell, this book – this common sense of a different kind – divulges why you, I, and females of every strip and age, torture ourselves when dating, when instead we should be standing firmly on a foundation of *male* common sense. It is intended to put our thoughts, emotions, and actions under the microscope, forcing us to see that in most cases we have the power to prevent the frustrations and heartache that can be associated with dating the infamous opposite sex. We are not victims – we make the bed we lie in. This is not a diatribe to bash men or put them down, nor does it present men in a negative light or portray them as the bad guy. In fact, it's a blunt, honest, and direct set of ideas that takes the focus away from men and places it directly on us – women. Truth be told, and whether we want to believe it or not, the problem is not with guys, but with us. We cannot control how men are going to act; they are who they are, just as we are. Our control lies in who we choose to become, and with whom we choose to share our lives.

Before we get started, I must lay down a couple of disclaimers. Number one: these thoughts and insights do not offer a discussion as to why or how relationships work, nor do they discuss the dynamics that comprise relationships. Number two: I am not a trained specialist. These are the views of an ordinary medical school student, albeit one well versed in the area of dating, and who maybe, just maybe, might have something to say that will change the course of history – dating history.

All About the Author

2

With a brand new degree in Forensic Chemistry, I am headed toward a career in medicine as a physician. My story is simple. I grew up in a typical American household. I have one older brother, one younger brother and three parents. My parents divorced when I was eight and my mom remarried when I was twelve (thus the three). There is much more complexity between these average details, however my family history is not the reason I write.

I don't recall the first time the realization hit, but for the longest time I seemed to have a huge neon sign above my head that read: Tools Welcome; and I am sure they flashed in a way that only the tools of the world could see. I have no idea how or when the words came to be there, but I can venture a guess that its presence had something to do with me.

My resume of dating experiences is quite comical, aside from the tears, heartbreak and endless frustration. I like to compare the majority of those encounters to impulsive buying. It's like seeing and purchasing a $300 pair of True Religion jeans at Nordstrom's. Never mind the fact that you have a dozen others at home similar in wash, cut, and style – you must buy them anyway, because in that moment no pair rivals them; they are too wonderful to leave without. There is no thinking, no consideration involved; you simply react impulsively. And this is how I approached dating. When I realized this, I also realized it was the biggest cause for the neon sign above my head because I had never stopped to think about who I was involving myself with. Each of my relationships would invariably go as follows: meet a "great" guy, begin dating the guy, realize he was a tool, and then be mystified why I had attracted yet another guy who was so completely wrong for me. It's extremely disconcerting to once again be standing where you have stood before – at the end of a broken road. Honestly, it felt as though I was dating the same guy over and over – different head, different body, different clothes, same guy.

I was falling for guys I barely knew, and I was deeply saddened when, one-by-one the relationships ended. I was becoming more frustrated and bitter toward the opposite sex, and I'd begun to notice how my feelings of inadequacy had grown, over time, and my confidence had diminished. It was time I focused on me. I knew in my heart I needed a break, and finally, I decided to go into dating hibernation. This meant no dates, no distribution of the phone number, no crushing on cute guys at the gym, nothing! It was an appropriate time to duck away from the dating scene. I needed to focus on me and the opposite sex would have been a complete distraction.

As I was going through this, friends often tried to provoke an early awakening of my sleeping dating self; however, I wouldn't concede. The hiatus was difficult, but what I learned would never have come to me, without the clarity this pause provided. I awoke from my nine-month abstention from men with the old neon 'Tools' sign permanently off – I had found the answer to why I'd been so lost in the realm of dating. It was simple, in fact, it was more than simple. Come to think of it, it was just plain ol' common sense.

Setting The Stage

3

A few nights ago, I and four friends were enjoying each other's company, as well as a bottle (or two) of pinot grigio. The others present were Krista, Paige, Riley, and Emily, the reason for the get-together. We were spread out in the living room of the two-bedroom home Riley and Ems share.

The inside of their small, quaint home looked as it always does. The walls of the living room were light blue (they have also been yellow, orange, pink, and lilac) and were covered with arrangements of pictures, which added warmth to the overall feel of the house. The living room stood in stark contrast to the rest of the home, with its empty, and still-untouched barren taupe walls, displaying the awful decorative taste of the previous renters.

Just to the left of the hall leading to the bedrooms, there was a large painting of five stick-figure girls, all holding hands, standing below a golden sun and a blue sky. Most of the painting – hidden by furniture, stacks of used textbooks and wall hangings – gave the appearance of five smiling, floating faces peeking over the top of the couch.

To the right of the front door was the kitchen which used to go unnoticed most of the time, but that night caught my eye. Normally the avocado-colored appliances stood against mustard-yellow walls that screamed of the 1970s; but its vibrant new coat of paint, which resembled the shade of pink bubble gum, somehow made the home appear younger.

Between the entry and the kitchen, hanging not entirely straight was a white board that was hardly white at all. It was cluttered with scribbles in Riley's handwriting, notes and messages in which she had attempted, in different ways, to cheer up Emily.

I thought about Emily. I knew all too well what she was feeling at this very moment. Within seconds of seeing the writings, I saw images of myself, and vividly recalled all the times I, too, had felt the heartache. Suddenly I saw myself not in the blue-walled living room, but in my own bedroom lying on the bed crying by myself; I was in a deserted chemistry lab being consoled by a friend; I was sitting on a bench with my hands on my forehead, wondering why I allowed myself to feel so hurt by another guy. These images were moving across my mind, leaving as quickly as they came, only to be replaced by another.

A tight hug from Krista shut off the torrent of unpleasant remembrances, and I asked, "Where's Emily?" She simply nodded her head in the direction of the hallway where the two bedrooms were located and I knew I would find our friend somewhere beyond her closed bedroom door. What was she feeling? Was she lying on her bed, crying by herself? Was she sitting on the floor, curled in a ball, her face wet with tears?

Ten minutes passed, then twenty, and she was still in her room. In fact, it wasn't until we were all pouring our second glass of wine that Emily finally came strolling out to join us in the living room. Despite her attempts to freshen up, her eyes – bloodshot and puffy – still told the truth – she had been crying.

It had been over three weeks since she had been dumped, and she was still completely mystified as to why the relationship ended. We listened for hours as her emotions and thoughts went up and down like a sinusoidal wave. At times she would vent her feelings of frustration, wondering why her ex-boyfriend didn't want to be with her. At other times her sorrow and mourning would turn callous as she expressed feelings of anger, saying many times that she was better off without him. At one point I think I even heard her mumble, "He did me a favor by breaking things off." Then at still other times, when her vulnerability got the best of her, her pain turned inward and her feelings of rejection led her to reflect upon every inadequacy within her, she felt had caused the breakup. My heart sank when she began to verbally list those reasons out loud.

As I was listening to her dissect the ins and outs of her broken relationship, I had a thought. There, sitting before me, was this beautiful, intelligent, and confident young woman who had the world at her fingertips. I sat watching her for a moment as she tried to soak up the inspirational comments my friends were throwing her way, and I couldn't help but wonder whether this conversation was really helping her. I mean, was hearing a group of young women bash a twenty-five year old immature boy making her feel better about the fact that he, for whatever reason, didn't want to be with her? I took a gamble on this question and answered to myself, "No."

Without taking a world poll, it is safe to say that very few people enjoy experiencing rejection. In my own cases, I have also felt a great deal of inadequacy. Truth be told, it is easier to internalize that rejection and search for inadequacies, than it is, frankly, not to give a damn.

That night with my friends, I realized that if I was going to help Ems overcome her feelings of rejection and inadequacy, it wasn't going to come by me telling her what, deep-down, she already knew. I had to take a different approach. You see, Emily was taking this breakup unusually hard because she was seeing herself through the eyes of an ex-boyfriend who no longer wanted her. If I was going to make a difference at all, I had to get her back to a place where she could see herself through her own eyes.

So that is what set the eventual emergence of this pamphlet in motion. This is where the idea was born. It all began with a bottle of wine, five young ladies, and my sense of being fed up with watching friend after friend search for inadequacies within themselves that never existed in the first place.

The Games We Play

4

When I think of games and the ones that are enjoyable to play, I am often reminded of my childhood. Just desperate to be included, I often agreed to play games with my older brother and his friends without ever really knowing what I was getting myself into. On one occasion at the age of ten, I found myself searching and searching our neighborhood for them in a game of hide-and-seek, where after an hour of searching with no finding, I finally gave up and went back home. I later learned that they had jumped the neighborhood fence, gone to a girl's house and argued later that, in their version of the rules, her home was fair game for hiding. I had no idea the area of play included five major blocks of the neighborhood. Apparently, I just didn't know the rules.

Why in relationships do we feel it necessary to play games? I mean doesn't that automatically set one of the two individuals up for disappointment? In typical fashion games have a winner and a loser. But why then would we want to turn a relationship into a game that will inevitably produce one winner and one loser?

The idea of games came up as I was in the midst of dishing my two cents to Emily. From her most recent relationship, she knew one of the games all to well, since she chose to play along. Its goal: try as hard as you can for as long as you can to resist showing feelings or emotions toward the other. Emily believed if she showed too much of her true feelings, her crush – her soon to be boyfriend – would have been scared away by her honesty. So instead, she fed into yet another game: *It's all about the Chase*, and continued for weeks to pretend her feelings for him were nothing more than a small crush.

As I considered what she was telling us, I had a thought. Maybe the reason she was still hurting wasn't because of her ex-boyfriend's games (after all – from the beginning, she was fully aware he played them), but because, deep-down, she allowed him to play games with her for months without her ever really knowing the rules. Allow me to explain.

Although it can be true that when two people first meet, games can be an enjoyable teaser that leaves both wanting more of the other, I am inclined to believe this only holds true when both participants acknowledge the rules by which they are playing. In Emily's case, her ex not only initiated the game, he created it as well. He set the stage. He made the rules. Yet should he be blamed for her heartache? Don't get me wrong – no one is really at fault when a relationship ends; it is just a matter of two people not meant to be. But as far as Emily was concerned, in her relationship she never stopped to so much as read the directions (the many signs he was giving), or bother to ask what in fact the rules of his dating game were. Maybe her lack of communication of her true feelings was an indication to him they were on the same page. During the course of their few months together, he saw their relationship as casual; but, failing to understand, she saw their relationship as more. Truth of the matter is, her lack of understanding for what she was signing up for with him, left her vulnerable to a heartbreaking game.

Going back to our idea of common sense, isn't this situation in need of just that – common sense? For any major decision we make in life, common sense would direct us to explore all possible options before a conclusion is made. This should be true for dating as well.

While it may not be wise to divulge passionate feelings too soon, it is okay, to do your own research in the first few weeks by casually poking around in conversation to find out where your potential new beau is *mentally*. The goal is to determine if you and he want the same thing from the dating scene. In other words, if you are ready to commit yourself to a long-term relationship, it would be a waste of time to date a guy who is only looking to play games, rather than settle down.

This was the case in Em's situation. Her ex-boyfriend was looking to play and casually have a good time, while she wondered when she was going to meet his family. She was so taken by him that she never for a moment stopped to ask, 1: what she was getting herself into, and 2: what the rules to this game she found herself playing with him were.

Common Sense Thought: If you are accepting an invitation to engage in a dating game, know the rules before you begin.

 You're Not Five  Anymore So Stop Pretending

5

As I continued my blunt, matter-of-fact approach to helping Emily move on, I couldn't help but see the looks of utter confusion my friends were throwing my direction. They were shocked – as was I – at how bold my advice had become. It wasn't as though I was tired of hearing Emily expressing her sorrow's; that wasn't the case at all. It had nothing to do with Emily, and everything to do with my own frustration as I watched yet another beautiful, smart, talented young woman put herself down because of a relationship that, for so many reasons, just didn't work.

I was about to put my rambling to an end when Emily, through a mass of tissues wiping liberally at nose and eyes, managed to sarcastically say, "Please Meg, tell me how you really feel." Then, with a smile and a sigh, she asked me to continue to shed light on her breakup situation.

Emily and I first met her ex-boyfriend while shopping one afternoon at Nordstrom's. While I perused the Mark Jacob bags I had no business looking at since my medical school education costs hovered over my head, a handsome, tall, charming, and clearly confident gentleman approached Emily. For me, aside from his great smile, the gorgeous face, and the muscular build, there was something about him that I didn't care for; he seemed the Eddie Haskell type. He asked Emily if she could offer her opinion on the two ties he was contemplating purchasing. After twenty minutes of shameless flirting, the two exchanged phone numbers and their courtship began. They saw each other casually in the beginning, and from all of her friends' perspectives, Emily seemed to be falling hard. This was confirmed to me a few weeks later.

I found myself staring across the dinner table at Emily's new boyfriend at an Asian restaurant he'd chosen. The two of us sat alone trying to make conversation after Emily and Riley had excused themselves to use the restroom. Emily has always had impeccable timing, a true knack for waiting until just the wrong moment to do or say something. This time, I had just taken a sip of water, rendering me unable to speak, unable to offer companionship on her momentary departure. Riley, however, immediately agreed to join her and jumped out of her chair to follow. This left me to sit alone with Emily's date.

I kept sipping my water, not because I was thirsty, but because it gave me something to do to avoid the awkward silence we were left with. Soon, my empty water glass was ringing with a slurping sound that was beginning to attract the attention of other customers sitting nearby at adjacent tables. When I realized I was no longer sucking water, but air, I conceded the point and lowered my glass.

You have to say something. Ask him how he and Emily met. No, that won't work – you were there. Ask him how things are going with Emily – lame – but it's better than saying nothing.

"So, how are things with you and Emily?" I asked. The quickness of his response and his eagerness to answer the question led me to believe he had anticipated my asking. I found, however, I was not so eager to hear his response.

"Things are going well. It's nice to finally meet a female who is just as uninterested in a serious relationship as I am – someone who doesn't expect too much from me. But I am sure you already know this; you are after all, one of Emily's best friends."

But the thing was, I didn't know this. Were we talking about the same Emily? The same Emily whom for years has dreamt about the man she would marry, and had every detail minus the groom sorted out for her wedding day? The same Emily who just days prior had told us this new boyfriend was someone she could really be herself around? I must have heard him wrong. Maybe he'd said he was happy to finally meet a girl just as *interested* in a serious relationship as he. But he couldn't have; he clearly stated she expected little from him. My Emily, whom I had been friends with for years, was not the same Emily this guy was talking about.

He stared at me, waiting for a response I was not going to give. I assume by what he said next, that he recognized the confused look on my face, and felt uncomfortable revealing something I clearly knew nothing about.

"Both your wine and water glasses are empty. Let's see if I can track down our server."

He scanned the restaurant, looked for our waiter, and avoided eye contact with me. From the expression on his face, I thought he had finally caught a glimpse of him, but instead saw Emily and Riley walking back to the table. Although our conversation was already over, I made a mental note to talk to Emily about it at the first opportunity.

Four days passed and I was still unable to tell Emily about my awkward conversation with her boyfriend. Frustration set in as his words kept reverberating in my head. I wanted to wait for the moment when she and I were alone; however, seeing this was unlikely to happen, I knew I would have to bring it up the next time she and I were together – alone or not.

"Hey Meg," Emily casually asked me in the paint aisle of Home Depot, "What do you think of this color blue for the living room walls? I know it's a little bright, but it's not nearly as bright as the orange they're painted now."

"Why are you pretending to be someone you are not with this guy you are dating?"

I couldn't help it – the question just soared out of my mouth. One second I was trying to envision what her living room walls would look like in that particular shade of blue, and the next I was accusing her of being fake with her boyfriend. All four of the girls I was with turned and looked at me. I hadn't meant to ask her then and there. In fact, I don't think I could have picked a more awkward time and place to bring up the conversation I had with her boyfriend, but I couldn't help it – the words just slipped out.

Emily's response – "I don't know what you are talking about," came in a tone that reflected both shock, as she seemed quite surprised to know that someone had learned her secret, and a bit of naiveté, in hoping her response alone would satisfy my inquiry. But I would not let it go, and as casually as I could, I explained the conversation her boyfriend and I had that night at the restaurant.

Emily didn't know what to say in response. I was ready for her to get upset, ready to hear her yell at me for my inappropriate timing, but she never did either. In fact, she answered me in exactly the opposite way I was expecting. She instead responded with a sense of relief, which came from knowing she no longer had to pretend – not with me or anyone else. For the first time since she had begun dating this guy, she could just be Emily.

Why is it that while dating, our wants and needs take a back seat to the wants and needs of the boy we are interested in? I mean, at what point do we allow ourselves to become second to the guy? I was so confused by this; I just couldn't understand why we allow ourselves to transform into someone we're not, just to satisfy the qualities we think a particular

20

guy is looking for. It is an almost robotic reaction. He says he's not looking for anything serious, and boom, neither are we. He has an independent/rocker style, and we exchange our J.Crew sweaters and Banana Republic pants for skinny jeans and Converse. None of it made sense.

When asked, Emily had no idea why she pretended to be someone different when she was around him, but supposed since she was so taken aback by his charm and good looks, she simply wound up putting him on a pedestal even she had trouble reaching. She'd wanted so badly to be with him, she molded herself into someone she thought he wanted. However, while she was pretending to be someone she was not, and thinking she was providing him with what he needed to stay happy in their relationship, she was unknowingly denying herself what she needed to be happy.

Can it be that the solution to this is as easy as simply not pretending? Can't the solution be that if you don't pretend to be someone you are not, you minimize your chance for heartache, because you avoid a handful of relationships you were never meant to be in, in the first place? Emily got her heart broken because she involved herself in a relationship that, for so many reasons, was never going to work. Eventually, her true self emerged and she could no longer agree to let her real needs go unattended. She was exhausted trying to keep up a relationship she was never really a part of. After all, from the outset it was simply a pretend version of herself who'd dated the guy.

While sitting with my four friends in the blue living room, discussing the heartache Emily was trying to overcome, I began telling them about my dating hiatus. Although it would appear my reasoning for walking away from the dating scene was due to the overwhelming number of "tools" I was meeting, there was an underlying cause for my decision I hadn't shared with anyone before then.

I began explaining to them that over a period of time, I'd come to realize I was losing myself in the guys I was dating. I was a pretender through and through, without ever knowing it. I had slowly started picking up habits I never had before – transforming into someone who resembled a handful of people – none of them me. Let me explain.

With each guy I dated, my personality would change to suit his needs, but, because I was blinded to this, I never thought to change back to my original self when the relationship ended. In other words, while beginning to date someone new, my personality resembled a bit of me plus a bit of the guy I had dated previously. This process kept repeating until I noticed my personality had become an accumulation of many versions of a pretend me – none truly me. I was no longer the same person. This, along with other reasons, is why I was attracting so many wrong guys. I mean, how was the right guy going to ever find me if mixed up in various pretend versions of me, even I couldn't find the real me? The only solution I could offer myself was to rediscover exactly who I was, exactly what I wanted out of life, and exactly what I needed before I could step a foot back into the realm of dating. I needed to find me again.

Once I discovered the problem and learned how to fix it, I wondered why it had taken me so long to figure out, since, obviously, it was only a matter of common sense. How can anyone find a true, meaningful relationship when they are pretending to be someone else? Hollywood is a perfect example of this. It seems to me the divorce rate amongst actors is high because they get paid to pretend to be someone other than themselves. And in due time their true self becomes lost, even to themselves. In a way, the same thing happened to me.

The girls were a bit shocked after hearing this. Emily looked relieved. She looked as though she was comforted by my honesty and vulnerability, realizing maybe there was validity in my advice.

I truly believe knowing who you are and what you are about is key to being happy in a relationship. If you know who you are and are therefore not willing to sacrifice it for anyone, you avoid the possibility of having relationships that threaten your true self. It's about having confidence – believing in what you have to offer, owning who you are, and never for a moment losing sight of either. If common sense has its way, then the days in which we pretend to be someone other than ourselves can be left in the past for good, only a part of our childhood memories – a time when we were allowed, without risk of consequences, to play make-believe and pretend to be whoever we chose to be.

Common Sense Thought: If you find you are pretending to be someone other than yourself for the sake of a relationship, then that relationship is probably not meant to be.

The Red Flags Are Your First Chance to Walk Away

6

The smell of takeout as Paige and Riley walked in reminded me how hungry I was and how desperate I was to leave my current company. For the twenty minutes they were gone I tried participating in a discussion the other two girls were having about fad diets; however, I was highly uninterested. Instead, I stared at the painting of myself and the other four girls in stick-figure form which was now mostly blocked and out of view. Krista, who had been studying art for years, painted it the day Riley and Emily moved in. Although it was meant to be painted over once a color selection was chosen for the room, the painting was too sweet to cover. Preserved, it was now framed with an assortment of random objects super-glued to the wall, which had accumulated over the years. I searched for the Jack Johnson concert ticket I'd recently added, but it was blocked by stacks of textbooks swarming with red sticky tabs. In fact, it looked as though a Post-it™ note factory threw up all over them. I couldn't help but laugh at what this scene brought to mind.

If my brain could be physically examined, more specifically the areas which hold memories of past relationships, I am confident its physical appearance would resemble those text books. I am sure I would see hundreds of red sticky tabs protruding from all areas, as red flag alerts I have collected through the years. I am certain a sticky would be stuck dead center on the horrible manners of one of my ex-boyfriends, as well as one on the ex who found it impossible to walk at my side, instead always keeping himself a few feet in front of me. And of course, I am convinced at least five red sticky tabs would be affixed directly onto the ex who felt the need to yell at his mom during every conversation they had. My mind is a library shelved with books of past relationships in which all have been flagged with red markers as evidence to why those relationships ended.

After having taken my hiatus from dating, it is interesting to note how few red flags are posted in regard to my most recent relationships. I suppose it's because now, fully aware of what I want from a guy, I no longer wait to let those red flags appear. In other words, it means I have walked off the relationship path I was on, and stepped onto a different path, a new path, that is leading me toward something better – something better suited for me.

When I begin a new relationship now, or see a friend begin a new relationship, I always envision two individuals standing at the start of a newly paved road. The two are not standing side by side, but on opposite sides of the street, however they are walking at the same pace, in the same direction, looking toward the same open horizon. For the sake of this piece, let's put you into this dating scenario.

In the beginning, when you and your new beau are officially dating, everything is great. You like him. He likes you. In fact, you are closing down restaurants because you are both getting lost in each other's conversation. Your world, for however brief a time, is a small candle-lit table for two, where only you and he exist. Things are going so great, in fact, that when, back on that imaginary road, you look to the horizon in the far distance, all you see is a long, straight path. There are no curves, no forks in the road, no diversions; there is nothing but straight road. Things are looking up and you are high on life as you think, "I could really see myself spending the rest of my life with a guy like him." But let's not kid ourselves – deep down you are really saying,

"I hope it is him I get to spend the rest of my life with."

However, after a few months have passed – after the butterflies of seeing one another begins to subside, and the good manners that come with the first few dates have begun to fade – the time when you really start to get to know one another – you look out along that road and you see it. You notice that on your side of the road, a road marker (aka a red flag) has popped up. In a real relationship this road marker can be any number of things. It all depends on what we want in a relationship, coupled with what we are willing to accept, or not, from our significant other. For the purpose of this situation, we will say the road marker you see before you is him telling you how he hates holding hands in public. Before you even realize, you notice that for a brief moment you both have stopped walking. You are standing alone on your side of the road faced with decisions. Your first thought is, you are okay with him not wanting to hold hands in public. In fact you tell yourself – or rather you justify to yourself – "I can live without holding his hand in public. There are so many other wonderful qualities about him that I am willing to live without this insignificant detail." This becomes choice one.

The second thought that runs through your mind is the exact opposite. You argue –

"I am not okay with him not holding my hand in public." This is choice two, and as you stop and ponder this road marker, you notice that while the road on his side continues going straight, on your side you have the option to follow a new branch. It is a road that won't include him, a diversion that leads away from your straight path; it takes you away from him. You are left with a decision to make. Do you chalk up his lack of PDA as a male thing and continue walking your path with him? Or do you cut your losses, recognize the red flag for what it is, because you truly can't imagine being in a relationship with someone who won't hold your hand?

The truth of the matter is, at some point we all face these tough choices, and regardless of how much we beat ourselves up over choices we've made, nothing will change them. However, I truly believe these red flags are meant to be just that – red flags – warnings, which offer us the opportunity to reassess a relationship. If we choose to ignore them, preferring to disregard the true worth that can come from them, then the road markers become road blockers, and before we know it, it becomes harder and harder to choose any direction other than this straight line. Understand, though, that any single red flag, such as a boy's refusal to show PDA, shouldn't automatically lead you to a breakup, but realize that red flags should be looked at carefully and evaluated to suit your needs. If you find you absolutely love to hold hands with your boyfriend, you should not have to sacrifice that pleasure. Once you recognize this is the case, then you need to consider that maybe – just maybe - this particular red flag appeared as a sign, alerting you to the hard fact that you and he are simply not meant to be.

Common Sense Thought: If you find red flags popping up in a relationship, it is best not to ignore them, as they are meant to help guide you in the right direction. In fact, ignoring them won't make them go away; ignoring them will only delay the inevitable.

Prince Charming Who?
7

When we are young, we are taught the basic rules of education. In kindergarten we learned the alphabet. In the first grade we learned to read and write. In the second grade, after we so proudly mastered the art of addition and subtraction, we learned multiplication and division. Nowhere during any of these lessons were we told of an underlying rule – *the exception to the rule*, rule. The sort of rules which include: i before e except after c, vowels are a e i o u and now sometimes y, anything divided by zero is not zero, it is undefined, etc. We reluctantly learned these new truths because they went against what we already knew to be correct.

As little girls we discovered – from our favorite fairy-tale princesses – that Prince Charming existed. We were taught he would one day transform from a frog, be our hero and rescue us from a tower, or even free us from a wicked spell by awakening us with true-love's kiss. As we grew older we learned, usually through experience, there is an exception to the Prince Charming rule as well; the exception to the rule is: he doesn't exist. Well, not really. Let me explain.

I have a story to share and it goes a little something like this:

Once upon a time there lived a normal girl who lived in a normal home, and lived a normal life. Her lips were pink, not brilliantly red. Her hair was blonde, but neither soft nor long. Her voice was nice, but she could hardly carry a tune. Her name was Jane, and like you and me, she had no fairy godmothers to bestow her with gifts, or royal parents to hand down a crown. In fact, she was as simple as simple could be.

Jane picked flowers in the garden but never traveled beyond the boundaries of their home. This meant she couldn't be tempted by juicy red apples or frightened by wolves. As an only child, she was never treated unfairly or placed below another. She was simply plain-Jane and would never be hated by an evil witch who envied her beauty, or a witch who would lock her in the highest of towers. Life for Jane was wonderfully simple, lived without danger and never knowing fear.

As Jane grew older she stayed close with her three best friends: Cinderella, Sleeping

Beauty, and Snow White. While the three of them were swept off their feet by their Prince Charmings, Jane wondered when a charming prince would come for her. She began to worry. She often wondered how he would find her if there were no dragon to slay, or even an enchanted kiss to bestow. Can a plain-Jane who doesn't sing in the forest or talk to the animals meet her Prince Charming? Would he still come for her if she had no reason to be rescued?

The fairy-tales we grew up believing would lead us to believe he could not, would not show up. But we were taught at an early age that he would come, risking his life to save ours, sweeping us off of our feet, and we would live happily ever after. Of course, this is all just sugar coated BS. In fact, I wonder if, as women, we truly accept the exception to the Prince Charming rule, knowing that in the fairy-tale form he does not exist. Or do we only pretend to accept the exception, while deep down, the young girl in each of us still longs for the day when, riding on a white horse, he will come and rescue us?

Emily often talks of her Prince Charming. She speaks of him as though he is wandering around the streets of Manhattan waiting for the moment to rescue her from the life she lives. While listening to her ramble about him, I couldn't help but wonder, what does she need rescuing from? Emily is a beautiful, intelligent, strong, wonderful woman. What is it about her life and who she has become that makes her long for something different?

All of these thoughts made me think, if Emily had never grown up reading stories about princesses who needed saving by a charming prince, would she still long to be rescued? Does she really believe that in order for her Mr. Right to be right, he has to come riding valiantly in to her life with a shield and a sword? I have a feeling she does.

If we look at this situation from a different point of view, using a different fairly tale, common sense would show us the truth. Let's examine the beloved fairy tale, *Beauty and the Beast*. Now I think we are all in agreement that a man, however selfish and rude, could never really be turned into a beast. Physically it's an impossibility – right? Common sense tells us this portion of the story cannot be taken seriously. So, if we are confident in believing witches and magic don't exist to turn a crude man into a beast, why would we be content to believe a woman has to be a damsel in distress for Prince Charming to arrive? If you are of the notion that your Prince Charming does exist, you must at least recognize that the Fairy Tales have got the circumstances wrong.

There is no one in this world who believes in true love more than I. I *believe* in love. But I'm also a strong, independent, educated woman who neither wants, nor needs to be rescued. Rather, I need simply to be found. Does this mean I am not entitled to the same fairy-tale ending as the damsels in distress?

Common sense tells us believing in a fairy tale will only lead to disappointment, as it is improbable any would come true. I believe every woman deserves happiness and a wonderful man with whom she can share the rest of her life. However, I don't believe the "happily ever after" must come dramatically, and in the manner we learned to expect so long ago.

No, instead Prince Charming waiting to find you just as you are waiting to find him. He is a man who will protect, love, cherish, and adore you. He is a man you, in turn, will protect, love, cherish, and adore. He may be a banker, a lawyer, or even be the young man you sat next to in a college history class. He could be anyone, anywhere.

Again, I have a story to share and it goes a little something like this:

Once upon a time there lived a normal girl who lived in a normal home, and lived a normal life. Her lips were pink, not brilliantly red. Her hair was blonde, but neither soft nor long. Her voice was nice, but she could hardly carry a tune. Her name was Jane, and like you and me, she had no fairy godmothers to bestow her with gifts, or royal parents to hand down a crown. In fact, she was as simple as simple could be.

Jane picked flowers in the garden but never traveled beyond the boundaries of their home. This meant she couldn't be tempted by juicy red apples or frightened by wolves. As an only child, she was never treated unfairly or placed below another. She was simply plain-Jane and would never be hated by an evil witch who envied her beauty, or a witch who would lock her in the highest of towers. Life for Jane was wonderfully simple, lived without danger and never knowing fear.

As Jane grew older she stayed close with her three best friends: Cinderella, Sleeping Beauty, and Snow White. While the three of them were swept off their feet by their Prince Charmings, Jane wondered when a charming prince would come for her as well. She began to worry. She often wondered how he would find her if there were no dragon to slay, or even an enchanted kiss to bestow. Can a plain-Jane who doesn't sing in the forest or talk to the animals meet her Prince Charming? Would he find her if she had no reason to be rescued?

Jane knew if she wanted to meet her true love, she, like her friends, would have to be patient. However, instead of waiting for him by picking berries, making pies, or eating apples offered by strangers, Jane decided to wait for him in the most peculiar of ways. Unlike her friends, she decided to leave home, get an education, find a career, live independently and meet him while he was doing the same. As far as she was concerned, there was no need for her to be rescued, or to twiddle her thumbs as she gazed out a window in the highest of towers. Instead, Jane would meet him when she least expected – and all this required of her was patience.

One day, out of the blue, while Jane was doing rounds at the hospital, in walked her Prince Charming. In the moment their eyes locked, she knew he was the one. With a towel pressed against his bleeding limb, it was Prince Charming who needed rescuing. Jane sutured his arm as fast as she could, since she could not wait to call Cinderella, Sleeping Beauty, and Snow White (who were now divorced, sharing a three bedroom apartment, and attending the local university), and tell them she had just met her prince.

Two years past and their day finally came. It was their wedding day. Jane and Prince

Charming became husband and wife and from this day on, lived happily ever after.

There will always be certain inalienable truths in life, and one of those is, the rules/lessons we learn will inevitably be followed by an exception. The exception to the Prince Charming rule: you don't have to be a damsel in distress for him to find you.

Common Sense Thought: If you envision your Prince Charming as a knight in shining armor and riding a white horse, then his damsel in distress, you, will be waiting a long while. Instead, live your life and wait not for the day where you will be rescued, but for the day where you and he will simply find one another.

Holding On to a Broken Relationship Won't Change the Fact that It Is Still Broken

8

I remember learning in psychology class that reflexes are innate. In other words, it is in our genetic makeup to jump when we are startled, drop a pan that is hot to the touch, or duck when something flies toward us. All of these things are done because they are natural reactions.

I wish there was an innate reflex for letting go of a relationship that has caused heartache – an innate response which would allow us to let go, just as we would recoil from a hot flame. However, it seems as though the opposite is true. When the ending of a relationship leads to heartache, it feels more natural to hold on to the broken pieces than to let go.

The evening I was talking with Emily, she was clearly struggling to let go of her recent breakup; she was trying so hard to hold on. Sitting there with her, I couldn't help but wonder, was she holding on because it was difficult to let go, or because for her, holding on was easier than moving on, easier than facing rejection?

In normal circumstances our body senses pain as a sort of warning to set the limits of what we can tolerate physically. If we subconsciously reject activities which cause physical pain, why don't we use this same mechanism for emotional pain? Why do we avoid physical pain at all costs, yet struggle against letting go of those things which cause emotional pain?

Personally, I find that it's easier to let go of a broken relationship than it is to hold on to one. In fact, clinging to a broken relationship reminds me of an unnatural force - like rolling a ball uphill, when all it wants to do is roll downhill. You can continue to push it upward for as long as you want, but the laws of physics will eventually have their way, and inevitably, no matter how long you resist, the ball will begin to move in the opposite direction. And all the while energy is wasted, spent rolling the ball uphill – spent holding on to a relationship that is over. And consequently, many positive things which can be learned from a breakup are often overlooked or go unnoticed.

During my talks with Emily, I found a contradiction in her. Normally she is an extremely positive, glass half-full sort of girl, someone who can find the silver lining in any situation. However, when it came to her breakup, she refused to see the many positive things that could come from it, and by doing this, she was denying herself the opportunity to grow and learn. As difficult as it may seem, if we stopped taking breakups so personally, we would find there is much to be gained from each and every one we go through.

We break up because something is broken within the relationship. It really is that simple, although we may refuse to see it that way. If we went our whole lives holding on to all the broken pieces of various experiences we were too scared to let go of, our neglected emotions turn into relationship baggage, baggage caused by our death-grip on to too much of the negative, and refusing to recognize too little of the positive.

As an example, I view my recent ex-boyfriend not as a whole person, but as a collection of all the qualities he possesses, which make him a whole. It's as if every one of his characteristics is laid before me on a long table, and I am allowed to pick and label the qualities I like and dislike. The qualities I like, I hold on to, looking for those in the next guy I date. For those qualities I don't like, well I just simply leave those behind and try to avoid dating someone who shares those same attributes.

This breakdown of pros and cons provides a great opportunity to discover the truth of what I am looking for in the person I am meant to be with, as well as the sort of relationship I want to have. The truth is, it's okay to have relationships that don't work, because at the very least they will help you come closer to finding the one that will.

I remember looking at Emily, and it was as if I could see, there in her hands, the broken relationship that she once thought was whole. To her, keeping a tight grip on those pieces was easier than letting them go and move on. She was perfectly content sitting on that couch, legs folded Indian style, protecting what was left of her broken heart and broken dreams. It was her dream to see him smile at her, for him to see all that she is; and in those dreams, she would be the one, in the end, he would choose to be his. I couldn't help but wonder if maybe it were her broken dreams, and not him at all, that made her so unwilling to let go.

Holding on to *what once was* only prolongs the inevitable, denying the opportunity for growth and knowledge. In fact, holding on to something that is not meant to be will hold you prisoner in your own thoughts, while moving on, although painful and hard, can only set you free.

Common Sense Thought: Holding on to the broken pieces of anything leaves you with only a bunch of broken pieces. Instead, salvage what you can from a broken relationship and dispose of the rest.

Don't Waste Time On Another Woman's Future Husband

9

On a random day of a random week, I woke up to my alarm going off. It was 5:30 in the morning and my eyes were burning, but I didn't pay it much mind; I had to quickly gather my things and leave. Weights were on campus at 6:00 am, and on my way I had to make a stop at the home of the guy I was dating. He was a collegiate athlete like myself and lived only a couple miles from me in the direction I was heading. It had been a couple months since we met and I was immediately taken by his smile and charm....

I could hear the rain pounding against the roof of the building I was in, and I watched as it cascaded down the windows, dreading when I'd have to run through the mess in order to get to my car. I was in the library with a student-athlete, tutoring him in a general chemistry course. The smell of old books and the sight of paint peeling from the walls made me curious about the age of the building. My student was working on a homework assignment that required little of my attention, leaving my thoughts free to wander. I turned my concentration from the shapes the peeling paint was making as it pulled away from the walls, and by accident made eye contact with the only other individual on the whole floor, who was sitting a few tables away. I wondered how I'd missed him before. I laughed at the awkwardness created when we found ourselves staring at one another, and quickly looked away. Within seconds my gaze was pulled back, and although he appeared to be studying once again, he was the only interesting thing in sight, and I soon found myself fixated on his arms. They were tan, very well defined, and, just peeking from beneath his sleeve, I could see a tattoo. I was drawn to its shape and detail as I wondered what sort of meaning it held. I couldn't, however, give it further consideration, as my focus was abruptly drawn back to the smell of old books, the pounding rain, and my student; my help was needed.

To my surprise, when my student left twenty minutes later, I saw the same tattooed design I had been so intrigued with earlier, except now it was inches from my face. I looked up and let out the same awkward giggle I had made before. This tattooed guy kindly smiled and said, "I couldn't help but overhear – you help students with chemistry?" I told him I did tutor, but only student-athletes. He smiled again: "Well then it's a good thing I play for the baseball team."

We set up a time to meet the next day on the same floor of the library. Once we got started, I was hard pressed not to ask if he ever attended a single chemistry class, because from the looks of utter confusion he gave while we went over some basics, it was as though I was speaking to him in a different language. However he tried to understand and I sympathized, as I knew the subject matter was far from easy to comprehend.

On our fourth meeting, when I asked him for the fourth time if he had remembered to bring homework assignments, graded quizzes or tests, he confessed the truth behind his lack of progress in this subject.

I was shocked to learn this baseball player was pretending to be in chemistry class as a means to get to know me. I wasn't sure how to respond because no male had ever put forth so much effort to become acquainted with me. I was flattered and at the same time startled by his vulnerability. I found his demeanor gentle, a quality I hardly expected from a strong, handsome athlete. With half a smile, I told him quite plainly he owed me a dinner for all the trouble I had gone through. He smiled back, relieved I wasn't upset, and took me out to dinner that same night.

Back to the morning my alarm went off at 5:30 am. It was a Wednesday, and this day was more important than most others. The baseball team was heading to Southern California to kick off a four game series which held the fate of the rest of their season. Knowing this, I dropped a note off on his car, letting him know I would be sending good thoughts his way, and saying how certain I was his pitching was going to lead the team to a four game sweep. I jetted out the door at 5:45 am, hoping my added stop would not make me late for weights, and certain by the time I was through, he would have sent a text message thanking me for the kind gesture. But he didn't text me that morning, or that afternoon, or even that evening.

By late that night I felt the pit in my stomach. I was studying a textbook on mythology, and after reading the same sentence a dozen times, I knew the information was leaving no trace of meaning behind. Over the next five days my ability to concentrate seemed to be absent from anything I tried focusing on. I hadn't heard from my baseball boy since the evening prior to their road trip. By now, the pit in my stomach was growing larger. I knew the unsettling feeling was caused by more than his lack of appreciation for my gesture. I realized that for weeks I had been going out of my way to do nice things for him, while receiving little acknowledgement in return. I was angry. I was angry at myself for putting so much effort into an individual who wasn't giving the same to me. Before he returned home, before I spoke to him again, I knew he was not the person for me.

With the slightest lingering sensation of a pit in my stomach, the image of this past experience faded, and my attention returned to the cozy living room with light blue walls. It was 10:00 pm and I was exhausted; I must have dozed off. I had not thought about this ex-baseball boy in years, and wondered why I had remembered him just then. I caught myself fixating on the many unnoticed things I did for him, knowing I would never again be so quick-giving to any future guy. I became distracted from my dark thoughts when I saw Emily in the kitchen talking to one of the girls; she had a huge grin on her face. From the looks of it she was either beginning to feel better, or was doing a good job faking it. As the two girls sat back down on the couch, all four looked at me as though I was supposed to continue what I was saying. I, however, had completely lost my train of thought and jumped to the only thing that came to mind.

Why do we waste our time on another woman's husband? I mean, eventually the men we date and break up with will one day be some other woman's husband, right? So why do we waste our time with them when we know they are not for us?

I couldn't help but notice the tears build in Emily's eyes, and I knew exactly what she was thinking. She often did kind things for her ex-boyfriend, and just as often as she did them, they just as frequently went unnoticed. Even though, deep-down, she knew she and her ex-boyfriend were never meant to be, she still wanted to believe that if she continued to give, his eyes would open, he would finally see what she offered, and the fate of their relationship would be changed. However, because they were never meant to be, because they are destined to be with others, he was incapable of seeing Emily's true worth. But instead of conceding the point, she continued to fruitlessly give, leaving her more and more drained. She was wasting her energy on an individual destined to be with a woman – just not Emily.

Putting so much effort into somebody who hardly gives the same in return, gets old quick! It would seem common sense should tell us not to waste our time on something that yields such poor results. I mean do we females value our time and efforts so little that we would waste them both on a cause we already knew in our hearts to be lost? And if this indeed is the case, I can't help but wonder, could this be driven by our seemingly perpetual desire to be *the one* for each man we date?

I brought up the idea of being *the one* to the girls that night. Emily shares, with many other women, the desire to be *the one* her boyfriend will ultimately change his ways for; *the one* who he gives his full heart to. While these desires are completely natural, I couldn't help but wonder where they stem from. I mean, do we put our efforts into an individual who will obviously not be ours for the long haul because we long for them to see the value in us? Or could it possibly be that our actions are unintentionally driven by a sense of competition we may feel toward the woman who really stands in his future? Let me explain.

I think it's difficult for women to ponder the thought there just may be someone else who is better suited for the man we care so deeply about. We get caught so in our own dreams and fantasies that the idea we're not exactly what our beau needs, gets obscured. But what if what we have to offer – wonderful as it is - is not what he needs?

Although the idea of there being another woman more suited for him seems unfathomable, the opposite also holds true - there is somebody out there better suited for *you* than *him*. It's all a matter of perception. While spending countless thoughts and efforts on somebody who will be destined for another woman, we lose sight of the thoughtfulness and care we need directed toward us. While you are busy giving to him, you have to ask yourself, who is giving to you?

Emily hated the idea that one day her ex-boyfriend would be softened and changed by someone other than her. She hated the thought that, unlike anything he ever did with Emily, her ex-boyfriend would, at some point, be with a woman to whom he would give his full heart. She saw him, for whatever reason, as a prize to be won, and she was convinced that if she could not have him forever, somehow that would mean she had lost. The thought of another woman "winning" at making him happier, despite everything she had done for him was, I believe, the driving force behind her wanting to continue her efforts, no matter what. Instead, with some perspective, she would have seen their relationship for what it really was – two people not meant to be – and she would have realized she was wasting her energy on an unchangeable outcome. She saw nothing of the truth and only what she wanted to see. And this is exactly where the problem lay. Emily's thoughts revolved completely around her ex-boyfriend. She never for a moment considered that his total lack of appreciation for anything she did was something that should not be tolerated.

At what point did relationships start to revolve completely around the guy? I mean, at what point did we start caring more about who else was going to get our beau, than the wonderful, and much more deserving person who would one day get us? It is almost as if young women have but one opportunity to find love, and if missed with the first guy they meet, their chances for finding it are lost forever. Again I say it's all about perception.

I felt it so important Emily understand this idea of perception, that she was viewing the situation from the wrong angle. As she was busy rattling off qualities she was sure her ex-boyfriend's future wife possessed and she lacked, I told her to look at things from a different angle. I asked her to list, instead, the qualities she felt her ex-boyfriend lacked, but which she knew in her heart her future husband would not. It took a while, but I think she finally got the point.

As women, we have to take control of our thoughts and stop investing them wholesale in men. We need to start making ourselves the first priority with our emotions, aspirations, feelings, and the like. More importantly, we have to come to understand we will not be *the one* for all the men we date; we will only be *the one* for one of the men we date.

Common Sense Thought: *If a guy is not giving you what you want in a relationship, walk away. It is more than likely you, just as he, are destined to be with somebody else.*

The Non-Fixables

10

Today we have the capability to fix anything that breaks. We have glue, tools, and duct tape to fix stuff that's broken. We even have tools that fix tools. We have medicine and surgery to fix a broken body, lawyers and legislatures to fix broken laws. We also have therapists to fix us when our minds aren't functioning correctly. So, in a time when money can buy any tool to fix any problem, it is no wonder we attempt to fix those things that need repair before we wash our hands of them completely.

Throughout the evening with the girls, aside from her broken heart, Emily was trying to fix something more tangible. In her left hand was a bottle of super glue, in her right a broken heel, and resting on her knee, the pump to which the heel belonged. Four different times the heel broke away from the shoe, and as many times she had attempted to repair it. While I sat watching her fiddle with the two broken pieces, despite the hours she invested trying to restore the shoe; I developed an urge to inform her of the obvious – the shoe was damaged beyond repair. I knew it; I just don't think she knew it. Since Emily had used every adhesive possible in trying to make the pieces stick, I couldn't help but wonder, why, in a broken relationship, do we try over and over to fix what is obviously broken? Is it because we refuse to accept, as with Emily's shoe, that our repairs only create a short-term mend to an unfixable break? Or do we refuse to accept there are just some things *we* are not equipped to fix?

While in high school, I had an on-again/off-again relationship with a boy. We were the typical break-up then make-up couple. Although at the time I wanted nothing more than for our relationship to work, it was highly improbable because as a couple we were unfixable. For various reasons our communication, our trust, our commitment were all broken, despite our many attempts to make them functional. Sorrow over missing one another when we were separated, fear of being alone, and a lack of faith in the knowledge we both deserved better, became the glue, tape and tools we used to fix the damage. The truth is, no amount of any of these things was going to provide a permanent fix. The broken pieces of our relationship were merely bandaged by our desire to want them fixed. What we never wanted to accept, again, like Emily's shoe, was that we had broken-up and made-up so many times; we were literally broken beyond repair.

As kids, when toys break, we lose interest in them completely. Even our most treasured and adored dolls, games, and trucks – once broken, will get discarded and wind up at the bottom of our toy chest. Even my Teddy Ruxpin Bear that never left my side as a child, retired to the top shelf of my closet when his bottom lip stopped moving to the music he played. What was broken in him was a non-fixable. I accepted him as damaged and simply began to search for something new to cling to. So with this example I can't help but wonder, is it possible to adapt the same mentality to a broken relationship, as we did as children with broken toys? Should we be asking ourselves: "What are the non-fixables in a broken relationship?"

Pragmatism and sentimentality would tell us anything broken deserves the chance to be repaired. However, common sense tells us something which requires the same repair over and over again will probably never truly be fixed. Just as the heel was broken at a point intrinsic to the shoe's functionality – at the point where stability needed to be at its strongest – it would be difficult, if not impossible to make the shoe like new again.

I sat there wondering why Emily didn't just discard her broken pumps and replace them with a new pair. Might she believe that if *she couldn't fix it she would simply tolerate the problem*? Did her broken footwear serve as a metaphor for her desire to fix her broken relationship? Let me explain.

Both her shoe and her relationship with her ex-boyfriend were broken at points pivotal to their fundamental functionality. As Emily's true self emerged from behind who she pretended to be, the glue – the reasoning for their involvement in the first place – no longer held up. She couldn't and shouldn't "fix" who she is any more than he could fix who he is. At the point when he realized they were too different to stay together, the relationship was broken. She avoided the obvious by creating short-term fixes by pretending to want something she didn't, by being someone she wasn't, but they were just that, short-term fixes. What Emily couldn't bring herself to accept, and her ex did, was that no amount of glue, tape, or any other fix was going to repair what irreparably was broken.

I am inclined to believe that as women, as natural nurturers, we crave what is broken. Hell, most of us are even guilty of being attracted to the "Bad Guy" (the guy who has a sign on his back which reads: *Save Me*, that only we can see), because we want to be the one who fixes him. But, accepting this, we also have to recognize there are situations we can do nothing about. Recognizing and accepting the non-fixables of a broken relationship will save us from future heartache. We must pay close mind to that fine line which resides between what can and cannot be fixed. If we cross that line and spend too much time on the other side, we just might wind up broken ourselves.

Common Sense Thought: If you find you are spending too much time fixing the same problem over and over again, more than likely it is a non-fixable situation. You have to wash your hands of it and move on.

Where Has All the Confidence Gone?

11

I often think about the women of World War II and the fascinating role they played in our country's history. I often think about the women of today and how their influence is marked in businesses, universities, and politics all around the world. I even think about the women who are in labor, giving birth, who hold the keys to our future in their very hands, and I ask myself, "Where has all the confidence gone?"

Our past tells us women struggled to break free from the political and social chains that held them. In other countries, many more are still fighting the same fight as those who blazed the trail for us. I see all the wonders our gender has created and I ask myself, "Where has all the confidence gone?" Today, American women are free, held down by nothing; yet still I ask, "Where has all the confidence gone?"

As my discussion with Emily transitioned toward the subject of confidence, I knew my words needed to be chosen carefully. I paused for a moment; I wanted what needed to be said to come out perfectly, but while I was thinking of how to delicately approach this, I could hear Emily in the background. She'd begun throwing out suggestions to the other girls as to how she could get back together with her ex-boyfriend. She was talking crazy, but my head filled with my own thoughts, which left me unable to digest anything she was saying.

I had always seen Emily as a confident, strong, intelligent and beautiful young woman, but, as she sat before me, I saw someone new. I saw a young woman with no confidence to speak of, desperate to cling on to something only her heart could see, but that was actually nothing at all. I got mad. For the first time while helping a friend cope with the heartache of a breakup, I found myself frustrated and angry. Without thinking I exclaimed: "Move on! He has!" Emily and the others looked at me with their mouths dropped open, waiting for an explanation.

While I certainly was not going to admit this aloud, I found I was almost proud of what I had said. It was the most honest, unfiltered statement anyone made the entire evening. My intentions were not to be harsh, I explained, but Emily did, nonetheless, need to hear the truth.

It is sad that there are females out there - Emily included - who have so little confidence in who they are and what they offer, that they wallow in misery over a guy who no longer wants them. And so I ask again, "Where has all the confidence gone?"

At what point do women lose sight of their own value? I look at Emily and can't help but wonder why she isn't recognizing the wonderful attributes she has to offer – why she is obsessed with how to change so that she can win back her ex. After all, I am confident he will not be the last male who will be interested in her. Deep down, Emily lacks confidence; she lacks a fundamental belief in herself. Truth is, until she sees herself as beautiful and wonderful, no guy will ever truly see those qualities in her either.

Why is confidence so hard to come-by these days? It's as if confidence were a scarce commodity, like grain in a third-world country. At what point did this become the case? Is it that we have placed so much emphasis on the perceived perfection in Hollywood and the stars within this industry that our own standards are set too high, affixed to an unrealistic goal? It's as if Hollywood has a monopoly on all the confidence in the world, and if you happen to be at par with those standards, then you can have a piece of the confidence pie. But what about the other 99.9% of women: the CEOs, the doctors, the political leaders, the stay-home mothers, the working mothers, the single mothers for that matter, and the battered wives who've gotten away from the abuse – why aren't young women looking up to them? And why, instead, do young women try to define themselves by the standards of an industry that is the cause of so much insecurity, and whose main purpose it is to play make-believe? To me, it is a contradiction. It's like trying to find truth within a lie.

However, placing blame and responsibility on Hollywood is a cop-out. Is Hollywood's glamour causing these insecurities? Or does our current society affect what Hollywood portrays? Which came first, the Hollywood chicken or the insecure egg?

I remember watching an episode of NBC's *The Office,* which I love; however, I was immensely disappointed after one particular episode. After ending the romantic relationship of co-workers Kelly and Ryan (where Ryan ruthlessly dumps Kelly upon notification of a corporate promotion), the producers later created a storyline in which Kelly faked a pregnancy in a last-ditch effort to hold on to their broken relationship. I was infuriated. How could they incorporate a story in which this female character used such ugly measures? Her character transformed from an independent woman proud of her Indian heritage, to a desperate female clinging to the past.

I had to ask myself what, if any validity lay in the actions of this female character. The truth is this character's actions were not a far cry from reality. In fact, there are women whose self-esteem and confidence are so diminished that they would and sometimes do resort to such desperate measures in order to hold onto something no longer there. They feel so inadequate that lies and deception become their only means to achieve their goal.

Common sense tells us that trying to find something real in something fake is almost impossible. Confidence does not stem from a perfect body, from a gorgeous smile, from the attention of men; it does not come from anything physical. Confidence is a state of mind. Confidence is being proud of the person you are; it is being true to the person you are. I have failed to see a confident woman who does not believe these things of herself.

After explaining this to Emily and the rest of the girls, their looks of anger began to dissolve. I am most certainly not trying to portray myself as an over-the-top feminist, promoting the idea that no woman needs a man to survive, however I don't believe a woman needs a man in order to feel confident about the person she is. So, when it comes to relationship breakups, how do we let go of the guy while still holding on to our confidence? Common sense of course! You hold on to your confidence by never letting it go in the first place.

If we put a numerical value on both our confidence and our emotions, we can look at this problem logically. The old saying: *don't put all your eggs in one basket,* is appropriate for this situation. Pretend for a moment someone you have recently met asks you to invest your entire savings in a business he is sure will produce much wealth. Hopefully we would all be smart enough to stop and think it over carefully before accepting all the wonders he guarantees. Chances are, the proposition won't produce wealth; but perhaps it just might. After sitting on the idea for a few days, using common sense and clear judgment, you conclude that while giving all of your hard-earned savings is not a wise idea, you can take a chance and invest a small fraction of what you have. In this case if it fails you won't lose everything, and if you win....

So you do it. Maybe it's a success; maybe it's not, but if it doesn't work, you're not ruined because of your clear-minded, sensible approach to the proposition. If we use this same concept, replacing an investment of money with our investment of emotions, we should get a similar result.

Emily had invested all her emotions, everything she had to offer on a bad proposition. While her willingness to give to others is a wonderful quality, it also prevents her from making wise relationship decisions. Emily gave 100% to a relationship, while her partner invested far less, if anything at all. In essence, when the end came, her loss was significant, while his was not.

Common sense tells us that investing too much of anything into something new and untried can be extremely risky. Why then would this not hold true in relationships? Why are we so quick to give our hearts to guys we barely know? The only answer that comes to mind relates to confidence.

With confidence, patience and clarity have a say in the things we face. If we begin to value the attributes we have to offer – see their true worth – we will be less inclined to toss them wholesale at the feet of the first guy who comes our way. In Emily's case, her lack of confidence caused her to gamble blindly on a guy she knew nothing about. Had she been confident in herself, confident about those things that make her so special, she would have quickly realized he was all wrong for her.

Common Sense Thought: Having confidence in who you are and what you are, before you enter a relationship, will prevent you from over investing in a risky business which has a high probability of yielding heartbreaking results.

 # Making the List
12

"Well," Emily said as she left the room, "On that note, how about some more wine?"

But it was late and clearly we were all exhausted, so I tried changing the subject. I asked Emily to grab a piece of paper and a pen from the kitchen. She returned with a grocery receipt and a pencil – the small, useless kind golfers use to keep track of their score.

I told her to write – even if she had nothing to write about – it didn't matter. I knew at some point what she was feeling would eventually come out, but in order for that to happen she needed to write. Writing is therapeutic – it allows your thoughts to be grounded in a place where they no longer echo within the curves of your head. Eliminating those reverberating thoughts was exactly what she needed. And before she even realized what she was writing, she'd begun to create her list.

When I emerged from my nine-month dating hibernation, my head was full of thoughts. I had given myself the opportunity to clear my mind, making sure my thoughts were my own, influenced by no one but me. I remember waking up one morning and wanting to write. It was as if my hand operated independently from my conscious mind. I stopped writing when my hand grew tired and found I had formulated a list. It was a list of qualities I wanted as well as needed from any man I would date – a written account of those things that would make me happy in a relationship. I knew that as time went on, and as I began venturing back into the dating world, my head would slowly become fogged again. Since I did not want to go back to the way I was pre-dating hiatus, influenced by artificial charm and good looks, I needed something that would keep me focused on my true heart's desires. Ergo, the list.

Often we want nothing more than to give our heart to someone, but in doing so recklessly, we lose sight of our happiness. There is an adage I love - quoted from *The Wizard of Oz* – and spoken by the powerful Oz to the Tin Man. He says, "Until hearts are made unbreakable they will never be practical." How true. Therefore, it is imperative we do all we can to ensure we are able to keep reason and logic close at hand when we begin to think with our hearts.

Making a list of both the positive things we hold tight to, as well as those negative things we have left behind, helps ensure we won't make decisions based solely on emotion.

We make lists all the time, for household chores, needed groceries, errands to run, etc., which serve as reminders of things we are most likely to forget, thus ensuring we do not. If we will make lists for simple daily activities, then why not make a list of the characteristics we want and need from both a relationship and a man? Besides, no one really knows when *the one* will come along. Who knows how long we will have to wait fighting through the treacherous world of dating before our number at love is called? With a list, the wrong ones become apparent, and the ones who have potential, they are just as easily recognized.

Common Sense Thought: Given all the things we look for as well as avoid in a guy, why not write them down so none will be forgotten? Write them down so you will always have a place to go, if ever our memory becomes hazy, or we have lost sight of those things most important to us.

The End
13

My reason for writing is to pass on why I believe I am single, and happy being single. It is my "philosophy for choosing me." I can't know if my thoughts will make any sense to you, or change how you see you; nonetheless, my thoughts are real, unfiltered, honest, and most importantly, common sense.

Although it took my heart being broken a few times before I understood that a fresh outlook, and a bit of common sense can make a vast difference in how to perceive relationships, it was, in the end, worth it. Wasting energy over a relationship that is not meant to be only causes you to lose sight of what is most important – you.

My mom always says, "Patience is a virtue" and in the context of relationships, it truly is. Have patience when it comes to love and be assured that if you use common sense and clear judgment, in the end you will find *the one*.

I left Emily and Riley's home that evening feeling exhausted and emotionally drained. I knew how Emily felt and wished only that she find her confidence again, but after I hadn't heard from her in a few days, I began to worry. I knew she wasn't upset; however, I couldn't help but feel guilty, since I had become the bearer of bad news that night. I knew that in her own time she would call – I just needed to be patient.

A couple more days passed and then, exactly one week after our fateful get-together, she finally called. She invited me and the other girls for dinner later that evening and I was elated to go.

When I walked into the home, and despite only a week having gone by, the atmosphere seemed different; however, the walls were still blue and our painting was still partially hidden by furniture and old books. I couldn't pinpoint what the change was until I saw Emily laughing and smiling as she entered the room. Her warmth, presence and personality cascaded throughout the whole home – she was the difference – she was the same Emily I had always known her to be.

That evening none of us talked about men, relationships, or the conversation we'd had the week prior. Nothing more needed to be said. Although I didn't know if my blunt, matter-of-fact approach contributed to her renewed, positive state, it didn't matter. She was happy and that's what was important. But, as it turned out, I got my answer by the end of the night.

Late in the evening, after I exchanged my empty dinner plate for a cup of honeyed tea, I wandered over to see if any new objects had been added to the frame surrounding the painting of the five girls. My concert stub was still blocked by old textbooks, and it seemed as though nothing else had changed; however, I did notice there was a new book lying on the top of the pile. The book's handwritten title: *Common Sense of a Different Kind*. Its cover was perfect, without the slightest bit of bend or deformation to it. The edges of the pages were brilliantly white, free of any markings or stains. But, like the used and dirty books, red sticky tabs stuck out from the side, marking areas of importance.

I opened the cover and found the first page, written in Emily's handwriting, was dated six days earlier. I looked around and caught her eye. With a smile she mouthed, "Thank you," which attracted the attention from no one else, and I suddenly knew exactly what I was holding – proof Emily was moving on. I was holding her journal for a new beginning.

Even though Emily never said, in so many words, that my matter-of-fact honesty was the reason she'd begun moving forward, I knew from her smile and nod that it might have had something to do with it.

My Final Thoughts
14

As I have said throughout, I believe in love, and that every woman deserves to find happiness in a healthy relationship. However to achieve this, we have to realize that we *deserve* to love, and we *deserve* to be loved in return.

I wish love, and the happily ever after ending we long for, was as easy to obtain as it is for fairy-tale princesses, but reality often has a different agenda. We must be patient, stay true to ourselves, and live our lives as though we have all the time in the world to wait for love. The moment we begin to force a love that isn't meant to be, is the moment we will ensure an eventual, and unnecessary heartache.

I like the saying, "Love will hit you when you least expect it." Expecting things in life only sets you up for disappointment, so don't expect love to arrive at any moment. Instead, wait for it, patiently, and embrace it when it comes. If I could offer only one piece of advice, having patience with love would be it.

Besides, being single is not as bad as you think. Enjoy what it means to be single. When you are married you will look back at your single life and recall a time when nothing but opportunity lay at your feet.

Don't waste your time on people who are careless with your heart; they are not the sort of individuals who will ever make you happy. Recognize the danger they posses and wash your hands of them completely.

Stop trying to change the men you date. Understand they can't be changed any more than you or I. You will have found the right man when you are able to love him for exactly who he is, and he is able to love you for exactly the person you are.

Don't worry about marriage or finding Mr. Right. They will both come in time. Believing in each is enough for now, and you must trust in their eventual arrival.

Don't waste energy on heartache or spend time fretting over a broken relationship. Overloading your brain with thoughts of why it ended will get you nowhere. Instead, focus on getting over the hurt by remembering it's the letting go that is the hardest part; after that, it is all down hill.

Be confident in what you have to offer. Bandaging low-self esteem derived from a relationship not meant to be will only cause unnecessary heartache.

Always use common sense to pick and choose your relationships. If the early Americans used it to build a country, there is no reason it can't be used to build a healthy relationship as well.

Allow time for the things you desire to develop. Don't rush into a relationship just for the sake of being in one. It's okay to be patient…especially when it comes to love.

www.ingramcontent.com/pod-product-compliance
Lightning Source LLC
Chambersburg PA
CBHW051710040426
42446CB00008B/811